OVE*

Months of the Year

August

by Mari Kesselring
Illustrated by Roberta Collier-Morales

Content Consultant:
Susan Kesselring, MA
Literacy Educator and Preschool Director

magic
wagon

visit us at www.abdopublishing.com

Published by Magic Wagon, a division of the ABDO Group, 8000 West 78th Street, Edina, Minnesota 55439. Copyright © 2010 by Abdo Consulting Group, Inc. International copyrights reserved in all countries.

Printed in the United States.

 PRINTED ON RECYCLED PAPER

Text by Mari Kesselring
Illustrations by Roberta Collier-Morales
Edited by Holly Saari
Interior layout and design by Emily Love
Cover design by Emily Love

Library of Congress Cataloging-in-Publication Data

Kesselring, Mari.
  August / by Mari Kesselring ; illustrated by Roberta Collier-Morales ; content consultant, Susan Kesselring.
    p. cm. — (Months of the year)
  ISBN 978-1-60270-635-4
  1. August (Month)—Juvenile literature. 2. Calendar—Juvenile literature. I. Collier-Morales, Roberta, ill. II. Kesselring, Susan. III. Title.
  CE13.K4723 2010
  398'.33—dc22
                2008050709

What is the name
of the month after July?
Can you answer this question?
Give it a try!

Did you say August?
You are so great!
Let's learn all about
month number eight.

5

This month has a total of 31 days.
There's lots of time to soak up the rays.

August got its name
from a man of justice.
He lived long ago.
His name was Augustus.

In August it gets
really hot outside.

Go to a water park.

Slide down a big slide!

It's back-to-school time,
but the fun doesn't end.
Share your best stories
with all your school friends.

Don't forget to play
with your friends this month, too.
Friendship Day is August 3.
It's fun for them and for you!

15

The second week is Smile Week.

Make sure your teeth are white.

Smile at everyone you know.

You'll make their days so bright!

17

National Banana Split Day is for making a treat.
On August 25, it is the perfect thing to eat!

August is Golf Month.

Do you know how to play?

Get in a game on a smaller fairway.

August is over.

What comes next? Do you recall?

It is time for September

and the start of fall!

Best Friends

Friendship Day is a good time to make cards for your friends. Draw pictures on the cards of fun things you have done together. It is a great way to show your friends how much they mean to you!

Banana Split Day

Celebrate Banana Split Day on August 25. Have an adult help you make the best banana split ever! When you are done you get to eat it!

Words to Know

fairway—the part of a golf course between a tee and the green where grass is mowed close to the ground.
July—the seventh month of the year. It comes after June.
justice—treating someone fairly.
recall—to remember something.
September—the ninth month of the year. It comes after August.

Web Sites

To learn more about August, visit ABDO Group online at **www.abdopublishing.com**. Web sites about August are featured on our Book Links page. These links are routinely monitored and updated to provide the most current information available.